NEW CONFESSIONS

Anthony Thwaite

ANTHONY THWAITE

NEW
CONFESSIONS

How do they know,
when they hear from myself of myself,
whether what I say is true?

AUGUSTINE

LONDON
OXFORD UNIVERSITY PRESS
NEW YORK   TORONTO
1974

Oxford University Press, Ely House, London W.1

GLASGOW NEW YORK TORONTO MELBOURNE WELLINGTON
CAPE TOWN IBADAN NAIROBI DAR ES SALAAM LUSAKA ADDIS ABABA
DELHI BOMBAY CALCUTTA MADRAS KARACHI LAHORE DACCA
KUALA LUMPUR SINGAPORE HONG KONG TOKYO

ISBN 0 19 211840 4

© *Oxford University Press 1974*

*Printed in Great Britain by
The Bowering Press Ltd, Plymouth*

PREFATORY NOTE

For some years I have been fascinated and puzzled by the figure of St Augustine of Hippo (AD 354–430). I was led to him partly by my reading of Synesius of Cyrene—that other, lesser father of the church, a Greek African rather than a Roman African, whom I commemorated in my 'Letters of Synesius' (*The Stones of Emptiness*, OUP, 1967). Towards the end of 1971, I began to see the faint outlines of the present book: an inner commentary on Augustine, partly in verse, partly in prose, which would be written in the margin, as it were, of Augustine's writings, but which would also be a personal book of meditation and trans-mutation.

The brief notes at the end of the book are chiefly pointers to sources. It will be obvious to some how much, or how little, I draw on Augustine's own words—from the *Confessions*, *The City of God*, the sermons, and elsewhere. To these same people, it will be equally obvious that I have taken ideas here and there from Peter Brown's classic biography, *Augustine of Hippo* (Faber, 1967), though Mr Brown is not of course responsible for the way in which I have metamorphosed and dislocated those ideas.

I am also grateful to Vernon Sproxton and Pat Miles, with whom I made a film ('Augustine of Hippo') for BBC 2 and Neyrac (Paris) Films in the autumn of 1970, visiting Thagaste, Madaura, Carthage, Milan, Ostia, Rome and Hippo. And special thanks are due to the University of East Anglia, at which I was appointed Henfield Writing Fellow for the summer term of 1972: during those ten weeks of leisure I wrote and planned a good deal of the book.

A few parts of *New Confessions* have appeared elsewhere. Section XXXVII was written before I had any notion of the book, though its position seems obvious to me now: it was first published in the Poetry Book Society's Christmas 1968 Bulletin, under the title 'Augustine at Carthage', and later in my *Inscriptions* (OUP, 1973). The penultimate section, XLIX, was also published in *Inscriptions*, with the title 'Retractions: Hippo'. Section XXXV (originally called 'Song Against the Donatists') appeared in *The Bulletin* (University of East Anglia) and later in *Ambit*.

I

It begins.
In the beginning.

Between the splayed thighs, excretion of blood and mucus, the miracle is performed. It is an aggrandisement, a conquering, and the passion is enacted, the victim punished. I am the triumphant blind bully of the bloody dunghill. Wreathed in my scarlet sin, badged with my grisly robes, I come among you, greet you with a cry.

Vast cloisters.
Redolent curtained rooms.
Sponge gravid with vinegar.
Creases and folds in the brain's wet linen.
Serpent biting its tail, baked to stone, become ammonite.

Thagaste, where among mountains a crossroads establishes a grid among drifts of sand: where nothing happened that I can remember happening. Or rather I became everything that happened to me, without remembering.

There is a row of red brick houses. A cello is being played by someone I call aunt, but who is not. I fall over, bruise my nose, smell vomit. Or that may have been later. Look, here is a picture of the house, the garden, the girl who helped my mother. I am there. I am no taller than the weeds and flowers I have indiscriminately plucked from that narrow garden. I was punished, I think, for that uprooting, but cannot remember how. I was uprooted, but that was not a punishment.

That one is long dead, but I am alive.

We skulked in a corner of the playground, near a manhole cover as broad and round and solid as a shield. Below it, we pretended villainies. I followed at the heels of Big David, who was seven. The path by the playground was made of loose chippings of green conglomerate, imagined gems. There was privet, and a room full of shoes. The tram that carried me home had glass steps. Waiting for the tram, I had my cap snatched off by a girl and thrown in the road. On Saturdays, I avoided walking by the house opposite our house. Jews lived there. They would force you to cook their dinner for them, my friend told me. I was chosen to present flowers to the headmistress on Speech Day. I wanted to excel, to be noticed. There was an order in these things, but I cannot see it now. Where do I belong? I was sometimes afraid, and sometimes am afraid now, and always with good reason. Or so I persuade myself.

III

Under the long brown crag running eastward,
Where the track comes down to olives, cattle, corn,
And the farms are husbanded and the families keep
Company with themselves, and peace is cultivated—
There is my place: or here, in a greener country
Where heaped fields stretch to the horizon
And the wind lifts the heads of the trees
And tosses them like horses, where hedges
Throb and rustle with pheasant, partridge, hare,
An ordered beneficence. But, here or there,
My spirit has no husbandry, no order,
Runs all ways raggedly, stumbles in sand,
Wades through tall lashing weeds, is lost in dunes.

The burden is in me, the heavy child of sin
Weighing my body to an ape's dull stoop,
Thickening the tongue, furring the eyes,
Falling down to the dust with the serpent's uncrushed head
And lying there unraised.

IV

Rationes seminales: they allow for the mutable within the immutable, so that we change and the world changes, yet all is the same.

But of course I would put it differently. I understand nothing of the physical laws: they perform their own operations without my understanding, and will go on doing so whether I understand them or not. In the same way, I feed on my memories without knowing what they are, without even knowing I do so. I dream, and interpret my dreams, and go on dreaming.

V

Pure is water, and a balm to many.
Pure is the sea: its salt heals many wounds.
Pure is the lamb that sucks its mother's teats,
White as mercy, whiter than mother's milk.
Pure is the steep mountain: in its air is found salvation,
And high on the mountain the tablets of God's word.
Pure is the black midnight of sleep without dreams . . .

VI

For dreams are memories and anticipations
Nourished on memories. The tempter slips
Into your bed and promises sensations
Half-known till now. Total the dark eclipse
Of the all-seeing and all-brightening sun.

When her thick stifling tapestry is spun
Your body is cocooned in its own dark,
Forbidding entry to all light but one
Struck smouldering from a quick and urgent spark,
An atom hot with elemental power.

It is the waking moment at an hour
When nothing fills the room but bloodless shades.
The watchman calls remotely from his tower
As day piles up and spreads, and light invades
Your dreams and memories and anticipations.

The transient shadowplay
Neither sent from heaven
Each makes his own
Lies heavily in sleep
Floats without effort
The day's performances.

Who has put to the torch
  citadels
Infantry in retreat,
The lawyer in his version
The miser, having buried riches,
The huntsman with his hounds
The sailor dreams of drowning,
The girl scribbles a note
Sends her a present. The dog
Follows the tracks of the
  hare . . .

Secret desires, ambitions,

mocking the mind,
nor flying out from temples:
when on the bed the body
and the untethered mind
enacting in the darkness

The conqueror of cities

sees flying javelins,
kings slaughtered, bloody.
sees the court, the high bench.
finds the gold dug, vanished.
harries the thick forest.
claws at the tilted prow.
to her lover, who furtively
twitching and barking in frenzy

All our remorse, misery,
follow us into the night.

Old reprobate, you described it all, but made no judgements. How could you, in your profound darkness? Where do they come from, then, these night-mists, these damp exhalations? And what do they tell us? Or foretell? My whole upbringing would have me acknowledge them as serious messages from beyond this world, only arcane because we lack the means to measure and assess them. Yet would God speak to us in such a primitive way? Does he seek to degrade us with lewd fancies, and then lead us by a thread of hypothetical interpretations, strung together like cheap beads on a necklace, to know him through these baubles? It cannot be. Yet they burden me with their beseechings . . .

I suppose he would have seen things like that. But what was he really dreaming at fifteen? Anticipations of warm mouths and secret hot places, touched and enjoyed? In some corner of Madaura, away from school, now frayed hewn rock collapsed in tawny sand, he saw a donkey fucking a girl: something like that. A crowd was watching, intent and giggling. He saw it later in a dream. But this time the donkey was himself, young Punic stallion staggering and thrusting. The girl was the same.

Lord, make me chaste.

X

But not yet . . .
                    There is still time
And the opportunities offering themselves
(For where is the initiative, who is the predator
In this excessive hunt?). Secretly I number them,
Catalogue inwardly their special favours,
Relish again and again their tender memories,
Or recollections that have no tenderness in them
But only fierce ardour and exultation.

XI

The adept tongue that trembles on the body,
Delicious in its searchings, moist with fire,
Accepts the flesh's wafer and the juice
Sucked from the swollen membrane of the grape.
There are ways of ecstasy, and ways, and ways
Among dark harbour streets, nocturnal, secret,
Where stalls are lit by flares and in the glow
Young faces shine with promises, a sweat
Of expectation, longing, guilty, poised
Above a drop that plunges to the sea
Where Carthage boils, from frying pan to fire . . .
I am stunned like an eel in a skillet with pure desire.

A promising boy, though weak in mathematics. He has imagination and a feeling for words. An able speaker. His efforts at Greek are sporadic, but with application he can show up perfectly good work. His handwriting needs attention. Altogether he should give a good account of himself at university.

. . . It is this that leads me to stay awake in the night's silence, studying how by choosing the correct words and exercising the art of the poet I can display to your mind a clear light, by means of which you can gaze into the heart of things hidden.

XIII

I have spent too long peeling and paring the skin,
Being skilful and busy with words—
The discrimination of words, the play of rhetoric,
The persuaders smoothing the way for quick profits,
The inscriptions, descriptions, repetitions
(Those on stone built into structures
That will last longer than the uttering tongue).
I admire the articulate, am indeed scornful
Of the barbarous mouthings of students determined to show
How far they are from the poised epithets of their fathers:
But now I look for a commerce beyond sermons,
Without texts or precepts or etymologies,
In some garden where theologies are mute
And the explanation is in the ripe fruit.

XIV

How many hours wasted at windows, looking out on changing trees, drifting clouds, a boy and a girl with their arms round one another? Restless, yet still: touching books, papers, ornaments: drumming fingers on the table, like an actor pretending impatience in a play. *Our heart is restless.* Waiting for a letter, for the telephone to ring, for a descent of grace, or good luck, or rain. *Until it rests in thee.*

A glum provincial with a thick
Outback African accent
Arrives in the capital,
A couple of testimonials
Stuffed in his dim baggage.
He buys a street-map, finds digs
Near some terminus or market
Where his fellow-colonials
Squat shivering over braziers,
Tell lies about their prospects,
Get drunk on cheap liquor,
And send home for more money.
In this quarter ('Lion Valley'
To humorous citizens
Who know where they belong)
Our comer-in sits waiting
For letters from his mother
And looks out of the window
At diurnal somethings and nothings
Till another day has passed
Unmentioned in his journal.

XVI

The abrupt convulsions
Of the new musicians,
The insolent stares
Of handsome queers,
The frank abandon
Of the latest fashion
In flaunting the body—
All leave me unready
To hold to my purpose
Or know what it is.

Among small ancient farms where every day
Morning enlists fields to be ploughed, stones to be cleared,
Fences mended, brushwood burnt, cattle and goats
To be herded from sparse patch to sparse patch,
And each day has its discipline and pattern—
From such ancestral narrowness I come
To find elsewhere no such conscripted labour
But talents scattered in a city gutter
And idleness proliferating like weed
In ways untended and unprofitable.

XVIII

Forms and observances. The tact of ritual, the courtesy of exchanges. The careful editing of rough matter. Everywhere I see such performances, the smoothing out of our barbarities. Not only do I see them, I participate: though provincial, I am urbane. After all, I found myself a place in the established order of things: I put out my sign, and it was recognized. But, putting it out, I put out something else—my small, fitful flame, the insignificant yet authentic tongue of heat and light. Not that it was ever my part to speak with the tongues of men and angels: fiercer men from the deeper desert did that, and my strongest passion seemed to be for reason. And I feed on the thin gruel of abstinence, keeping a head clear for whatever epiphany is chosen, and a body lean and spare for combat. But what if the rigour of the will is only the rigour of death?

XIX

It loosens the tongue, that swollen, unlovely
Instrument of rhetoric, licking the juices
Of grapes or bodies, indiscriminately.
Since I forswore it, I have discovered
Nothing in the thin liquids of virtue
But the same dull man stuck with the old brick wall,
Only now caged in conscious sobriety,
Controlled as a clenched fist is controlled
Till the veins stand out, straining like hawsers, the palms
Sweat in their prison, and, when the fingers part
With a moist, thudding suck, the arm trembles with joy
But only at relief.

XX

And what of you whom I have put away, put out of mind—except that twenty times a day, and more often in my dreams, you pierce me with your presence? It cannot be mud that splashes across my memory, remembering my second nature, which was you. But I must bury you deeper still, and leave the place where you lie.

There might have been a wedding
Some other year, in another place,
Blessed no doubt, a complete sacrament,
Just like the real ones that happened
And go on happening. There might have been
Such a joining, such a marriage,
Such a bringing and keeping together
That God himself would have approved.
(Though you would not accept such an extravagance,
And as for me—I grant you an emptiness.)
But whatever disposes such matters chose
To settle our pasts and our futures differently,
To go our different ways.
                                    We settle
For what we have, and keep our separate pledges
Made to our alien, ignorant partners, whose love
Binds us and separates us and will not let us go.

XXII

Harbinger, prolegomena to the great work: for almost thirty years I have travelled with you, but only as an outrider, a figure on the scene, an agency for the promotion of others. I must set off now, on my own journey.

XXIII

No one has known I have been in this city,
For twenty-four hours doing my secret business
Among suburbs preoccupied with their own secrets—
Silent betrayals, assignations, adulteries.
If I said that I saw my life suddenly changing
In a way that will have no room for what we have shared,
You would suspect I had found someone else
And was making elaborate excuses for a disappearance
To another country with my infatuation.
That would be a mistake: to suppose
Liberty exacts only gifts of selfishness
Or secrecy always shrouds something disreputable
Is to miss the will's strange armoury of chances.
I am committed to a choice I made
When chance suddenly threw in my direction
Dice that fell in unalterable patterns.
The web of subterfuge was broken and blew away,
And I was released to play a different game,
A role I never knew I was capable of.
I am an agent devoted to working out
The secret will of powers not my own.
I draw no pay, am not rewarded
With the unaccountable munificence that is given
To other spies. But what I do is dangerous,
Acts as furtive as theirs, meetings as charged
With all the possibilities of abrupt
Discovery, interrogation, death.
And now, as I leave the city late at night,
Among other travellers who ignore my presence,
I must tread with circumspection through fact and fact,
An alibi glib at my lip for every
Contingency tomorrow's dawn may bring
To ambush, and the questions on the road
I must learn to answer darkly, if at all.

Deviousness of collapse. Weeping, in the suburbs, arid, broken,
chest cramped with sour liquids, in extremity. Forsaken.

XXIV

Across dry gardens wrinkled leaves are blown
To lodge in corners where they stir and creak
Dryly together, like old men who speak

Only of what is dead and past and known
Too long for speech. I sit beneath a sun
Grown cold and white as a wind-whitened bone.

Somewhere a child's voice calls, a tune ascends
Through notes as shrill and liquid as a thrush.
Half of my life begins as one half ends.

A cloud moves. A weight presses me, is gone.
What would both lift and lighten me, yet crush
My spirit like a thunderbolt from the sun?

And all I have lost is suddenly made one.

He recorded in his book how it happened, how whatever it was—revelation or awakening—came to him, struck him down, made him new: how after that nothing was the same. It is the turning point, the still centre—all the other dead metaphors we use to keep alive an experience we do not want to die. Ten years fell between the conversion and the confessions. I sit here in the garden, at his recorded and recording age, and watch a squirrel worry the fallen apples of a good harvest. There is nothing left to gather. The dropped fruit will rot. There will be winter, and then spring. I read 'the self-portrait of a convalescent'. My sickness is a nervous tic in my right eye, and the doctor prescribes sleep. *Peritus . . . periturus.*

By the decay and succession of things the beauty of the age is woven.

    The salt at Agrigentum
    The Garamantian fountain
    And that at Epirus
    The Arcadian stone
    The fig-tree in Egypt
    The apples of Sodom
    The Persian pyrites
    And the Persian selenite
    The mares of Cappadocia
    The trees of Tilon

    Thrown in the fire turns liquid,
    In water crackles as if on fire.
    So cold by day no one can drink it,
    So hot by night no one can touch it.
    Quenches lighted torches
    But lights those that are quenched.
    Once lit cannot be put out.
    Sinks to the bottom but, soaked,
    Rises again to the surface.
    Ripe in appearance
    But dust when bitten into.
    Burns the hand. Waxes and wanes with the moon.
    Impregnated by the wind.
    Never losing its foliage.

XXVII

These quiddities, these inscapes, are foreign to me: I must transpose them. But in the transposition lies all the knowledge I have, and all the knowledge I have of what I do not know.

The observations of *otium liberale*.

The reticulations of the centipede
The ripe haze of the clogged orchard
The brief gamut of rain sounding in gutters
The moss still warm in the quail's empty lair
The thin crushed touch of gravel to the nostrils
The spectrum smeared on the narrow paths of snails
The wind heaving the canvas and bracing it taut
The pierced arrow from which stormclouds bleed light
The nipple rising in its stippled disc—
                                        Ask
What binds them in perfection, each perfect,
Distinct in harmony, joined in separation,
Poised to admit, administer, reject,
Supple in passiveness, precise in action . . .
                                    Question
How each maintains its place, follows its destiny
Through maze of choice, through labyrinth of error,
Unhindered in its rapt scrutiny
Of its own selfhood in its selfhood's mirror . . .
                                    Enquire
What chooses each one's scale and range, duration
In centuries or seconds, when each dies
Or each gives birth, where bounds are set to function
And how something of each survives and stays . . .
                                    Then praise
Your scrupulous, enquiring ignorance
That weighs, notates, equates and calculates
Through instrument and seminar to advance
Knowledge compounded of ciphers, digits, dates,
Curves of progression, graphs of incidence,
Footnotes to texts, glosses to notes on notes—
And in the end, triumphant, shrugs to advance
The notion that all this depends on chance,
A blizzard of randomness where each separate flake
Whirls in its own six-sided snowy quake,
Starting from nothing, ending in nothing, blank

As untouched drifts of snow, without meaning till
Footprints mark out the power of man's will:
Neat as the rhyme in perfect measured lines,
Technique ascends, the universe declines
To fall through holes in space that no one knew
Existed till professors told them to . . .

The reticulations of the centipede
Move effortlessly, thriftily, at speed.

XXIX

Step down.
        Under the pavement, under the thronged road,
below the weight of earth, the cave of origin
opens and claims its chosen one: *fons*
et origo. Water, wrapped and lapped,
in a stone chamber, cold and salt with tears.

XXX

This Certificate of Baptism holds nothing but the official calligraphy of a diploma, the copperplate of institutions, according to which we are born, marry, and die. Would things have been different if I had stepped down into some hygienic font or swimming bath several decades later, or had clapped hands like a Jesus Freak in a euphoric torrent of adolescent amorousness, lost and found? Instead, I yelled in my parsonical grandfather's arms and knew nothing about it.

XXXI

Where were you? I was where I always was
But you were absent or absconded. Who
Housed you or hid you, in whose unknown face
Did you assume the features that I knew
But did not know? And for how many days
Did you desert me when I looked for you?

I too was where I was, and looked for you
But you were elsewhere, out of sight because
A shade or phantom was the thing you knew,
Error of sight, of judgement and of place,
And I was distant to a seeker who
Sought everywhere but in my open ways.

XXXII

The prodigal returns, is rich with gifts.
Shriven and blessed, come home to his own sty.
Purpose is single, husks will turn to grain.

The shore approaches, the beaked prow drops and lifts.
God looks down from the sun and blinds his eye.
The prodigal inherits his domain.

An exercise of virtue, that unused muscle or useless appendix, atrophied limb and difficult translation. Rhetoric of volition, speech of will. Illuminated, mad. Henceforth politician of the enlightenment, custodian of the lunatic: patron of the Inquisition, rubric of the Reformation, scourge of the schismatic, prosecutor of the heretic. The bitter sea of humanity floods through the dykes. In its wake is salt.

Erudition. Admonition. Discipline. Or, looked at in another way,
Believe, Obey, Fight. The will is weak and often devious: it finds
stones in its path and trips easily, it looks for obstacles where
none exist. It must be taught, warned, and if necessary punished.
'From the canes of the schoolmasters to the agonies of the
martyrs' is a progression. What we have to do to those who refuse
to be persuaded may seem harsh. So it is. I do not pretend
otherwise. But consider the casuistries of these recusants, by
which they themselves excuse their own harshness, their own
fanaticism, their own violence. They look at history, and make
history their justification: certain supposed acts, certain presumed
treacheries. There were men, years past, who may or may not have
compromised with the temporal power: today, these vigilantes
would exhume their bodies and defile them. There were battles,
long ago, which—it is said—were fought to set such matters to
rights: today, these vigilantes would fight them all over again.
Other men say, in what they suppose is a spirit of tolerance:
'Let us put it to the vote—let us reconcile our differences with a
referendum.' But matters of faith are not to be settled by casting
a scribbled scrap of broken pot into a leather bag. To fight the
strength of evil we must ourselves be strong. 'Know what you
are fighting for, and love what you know.' Put on the whole
armour of God. And as you go into battle, sing. The vigilantes
have their own songs, wild ravings and rantings about the True
Faith. Very well: answer them with your own song.

Your vigilante brother
Is full of pious deeds.
He'll take his Catholic mother
And scourge her till she bleeds
Because her father's father
Was maybe short on faith
And possibly would rather
Have saved his mortal breath
Than stand with sixty others
In the hallelujah tent
Shouting to a God that bothers
About what Donatus meant.
O the wicked sins of the mothers
O the temple veil is rent.

Your vigilante stalwart
Enjoys himself at night.
Tying a rope true-love knot
May seem a mild delight,
But your vigilante ties it
Round necks and pulls it till
The victim chokes and cries 'It
Is true about God's Will!'
After which the poor old sinner
May have a moment's peace
Before a sword is in her
And she's bleeding on her knees.
O the true Lord is a winner
O God's Adversary flees.

'Now gather round, my bullies',
Your vigilante cries,
'We must revenge old follies,
And he who wavers dies.
Up with the true religion,
Up with the holy books,

The dove is not our pigeon,
Carry daggers in your looks.
For wasn't it Our Lord himself
Who said he brought not peace
But a sword—so take it off the shelf
And give your souls release.'
O judge what's true, each for himself
O you who joy in peace.

XXXVI

But the wounds. The blood not figurative, the cries not meta-phorical. An armoury of weapons and a cell of torturers. When a man stands up and says 'If necessary, we are prepared to fight', he is either drunk or mad. Or innocent. Never to have seen a human being kill or be killed is a gap in one's experience, but it can easily be closed, like the innocent eye. What he wanted to be done and what this involved actually doing—between the two lay a gulf much wider than the narrow sea he had crossed with such exuberance.

Filled with fear myself, I fill you with fear.

No one had told me this was what to expect:
The mouth full of ashes, still warm from the promised feast,
And the slivers of bone hacked from the offered beast
And the dry knot in my gullet not wanting to swallow.
No one told me. Released
From condign ambitions, from words of a worldly text,
I stand on this spit of sand, pointing north from home,
Stale spit sour in my mouth, the devils brought low
In front across tracts of livid disordered foam
And behind across still deserts, unsettlable waste.

Without dignity, without position
Except to keep upright, propped between day and night,
The refugees crowd wanly out of sight:
But I know they are there, unsummoned to the feast,
Without fire, without light,
In attitudes of abandon or contrition.
They have suffered: suffer: the losers, they pay
For their leaders' heresy, the mark of the beast
Branded yesterday, confirmed today
To go on suffering, until proved contrite.

Carthage, you too were brought low, garnished with salt,
A triumph of waste, defaced for your impudence.
I have seen our enemies burned for their vile offence,
Should find it just, should applaud the divinity
That has wrung the due expense
Out of that proven vileness. Scrupulous to a fault,
I measure the given word against the deed
And find the blistered child on its mother's knee
Wrings something out beyond justice: makes me bleed
For something unassurable, for innocence.

But I am committed. I accepted the thorny crown,
The stigma of blood, the word in the desert, the thrall
Banishing all but the doctrine that those who fall
Fall through the truculent will, gone wild and free.

There is no parable
Our Lord told that has set these scruples down
As I would wish them. Committed to this war,
I must accept devout belligerency.
And yet as the desert winds and the waves roar
Across this headland, I pray for some sure call
To deafen our hymns, to rise and drown us all.

Luther on Grace. Calvin on Predestination. Torquemada on Coercion. Newman on the Secret Power of God. A full billing, with Augustine's name among the small credits at the bottom: 'Based on an idea by . . .' Credit where some would say discredit is due.

> The baths at Carthage. Flesh and heat. Great robes
> To be cast aside to show the corpse beneath.
> Gold. Marble. Mosaics in darkness, darker glow
> Of reliquaries, plumes of candles. Strong-voiced,
> The Requiem treads down the ashes, prayers
> Pre-empt and empty out what justice means.
> Power is anguish to the trodden neck,
> Is exultation to the heel that grinds:
> Between them dust is blown to the four winds.

Let falsehood, once detected, bow its neck to truth made manifest.

You are with me in the night, as I lie awake and feel my age absorb its sustenance of vinegar. The streets still throb outside my window, reminding me of all my accretions. As I remember disputations, transactions, admissions, confessions, absolutions, I remember also journeys, searches, moments of abandon, moments of blankness. The smell of honeysuckle, the taste of figs, the sight of a lizard quick on a wall, the touch of sand under the fingers, the sound of the sea wind knocking the canvas. I am trapped by them all, moment by moment, until the whole well of myself is replete with them, the heavy liquid of selfhood. I flow over with incident and token, sign and experience. And in this flood of randomness, where am I but in the separate drops and moistures you have chosen for me, an amalgam of your mixing, an alembic for your experiment?

Night of commemoration and celebration, a triumph, a carnival. Heaped fires smoulder and explode on the swart horizons of a winter night, and the sparks are lobbed upward above shadowy and flaring trees. Dazzling, consumed in brilliance, fitful among the stars, driven to the perimeter of their own light, extinct. The faces of children are reflected in them, a pristine torrent, a former glory. Transfigured martyrs, clasping the once kindled crucifix, bow and topple into the purging rubbish. And the meadow is littered with spent tatters and smudged casings, soggy among nettles and trodden turf under the mist that elbows in through the deserted fields. The psalmists are silent, the prophets' mouths are stopped. The brief imperial holiday is over, and all the pyres burn level with the earth. Victories are vanquished, the dux is acquainted with defeat. The remembered smell of flames rises like grief to the horses' nostrils, and the imagined sting of smoke brings tears to men's eyes.

Small and unseemly memories of men discomfited, their trivial posturings mocked and proved fatuous. Is this my cardinal sin, to enumerate them secretly and glow at their number? They will never be the villains of repeated feast-days but footnotes in history, the scurf of scholarship.

Old lizard-face, gloating over the loathsomeness of sin, sancti-
monious adversary, apostle of the Manichees, slobbering in the
confessional. Spiritual teaser, *allumeuse* of the inflamed conscience.
Thus I recall you. Or that other one, so bland and reasonable,
inclined above the sherry glasses, nodding agreement at the
polite and deferential questions of ladies unready to acknowledge
even the existence of sin. You too I remember. For I subjugated
both of you. And I have my pride.

But there is a darkness beyond all this, and it still prevails. Beyond the smug indulgences of the *urbs*, beyond the indifferent justice of the *civitas*, beyond the pitiful gestures of the *ecclesia*, lurk the ten thousand gods, the ten million demons, the plagues, the devastations, the elemental disasters, the deepest and darkest nature of man. And the priests who dissemble it.

The countenance of God: is the muzzle of Baal.
His gifts are the udders of Tanit: flowing to our lips.
His sacrifice is comely: in the dances of women.

The countenance of God: is the belly of Baal.
His gifts are the mountains of Saturn: whose clouds shed fear.
His sacrifice is comely: in the slaughter of animals.

The countenance of God: is the loins of Baal.
His gifts are the knives of Vulcan: flashing like lightning.
His sacrifice is comely: in the blood of children.

Numidian mornings, when the sun is still furred with mist, cool for journeys. Beyond the city wall are neat fields sopping with dew, and hills that are this side of danger. Peasants are bent-backed between vines, busy among orchards. Far from the briskly trod marble of the basilica and the rough trade of the market, small birds bubble and clack in groves of juniper and pastures of myrtle. Or elsewhere, in a river landscape of glebe, copse, moorhen and kingfisher, unhindered yet possessed. But a tumulus looms across meadows, low burden of old sacrificial compulsions, plundered relic of vanquished theologies. Stone knife, bronze dagger. As the builders' men move in, under the hearth or by the lintel they uncover a stone salt-glazed jar, whose grimacing mask warns of a lock of hair, a handful of nails, a stain of urine, a pierced heart cut from musty cloth. The heat of the winter sun chills to an icy meteorite, as men believe in witches and old women die in fire.

XLIII

Arguments, purges, assassinations, invasions,
The Gothic disaster: so the dragon hovers
Unseen above your head in muddy dreams.
The potter's wheel spins on.

Unde hoc malum? From the Devil's tree
Ripe fruit is shaken. We tread Paradise
By slippery ways, pursued by eager fears.
The potter's wheel spins on.

The gospel of madness is preached by doctors. Both
Chance and necessity are blunderings.
A troupe of jingling pilgrims wails with joy.
The potter's wheel spins on.

The expelled are patronized with charity.
The unborn are damned before they reach for breath.
Go to the ant, but hear the termite eat.
The potter's wheel spins on.

The cricket chirps: the swan is silent, scum
Thickens across the river's slow descent
Through choked effluvia, discarded trash.
The potter's wheel spins on.

Occupied with affairs, busy with deliberations, something within
me dries at the root, shrivels to a slow and parching dust. There
is the world, and there it is: to be negotiated with acquired skill,
or plunged into and crossed with inherited courage. Which is the
proper choice, if there is still time to choose? For no doubt the
choice has already been made, or was made long ago, when I was
dully and dutifully making my conscientious efforts to advise,
exhort, chastise, illuminate, discriminate. Such small gifts, talents
reduced to a degenerate coinage by inflation. Men furtively bury
their wretched hoards in the footings of walls, under hearth-
stones or thresholds, stamping down the disturbed earth, easing
back the shifted masonry, secure as moles in their darkness, and
as blind. So it seems with my less ponderous talents, debased
small change that issued from no exchequer. When the treasure
is dug up, it is no longer treasure, but an obstruction to the
blunt hoe of a peasant I shall never see and to whom my judgements will be as unapprehensible as the desert wind that blisters
his trees and cannot be trapped or tamed or even understood.
And that hot wind is the same that has scorched my spirit to this
dry pinch of inert matter I hold between my finger and thumb.
I say to it, Arise, and the dust blows away, leaving my hand
empty.

If, of those two companions on Golgotha, one was saved and the other condemned, is my God indeed the God of Manes, holding the inexorable balance between dual forces? A duel between equals, never to be won? The play on words becomes a mad contest with swords, for every word I use can draw blood, and many a sentence is a sentence of death.

XLVI

The masons split cold marble with iron mallets.
The carpenters swarm over their wooden carapace like ants.
The wells are dug deep and girdled with basketwork.
The harbour is fashioned into the sea's embrace.
Below, the chips of mosaic litter new floors.
Above, the finials glisten over new roofs.
But everywhere nothing prospers
Unless the Lord wills it, of the house as of the city.

High on the hill the basilica shines in its glory.
Low by the sea the bollards capture the cargoes.
Columns are ranked like harp-strings by temple and forum.
Avenues strike like arrows to east and to west.
The market is busy with cries and acquisitions.
The workshops are quick with skills and intricate craftings.
But everywhere nothing prospers
Unless the Lord wills it, of the house as of the city.

Even the greatest of cities, Rome, is abandoned:
Her citizens come among us, fled from the deluge.
Where is a refuge, here or beyond the Pillars,
Safe from the envious swords, the curt invaders?
Rome is an emblem, woven into our banners,
Fading in sunlight, falling so as to prove us
Comfortless in our error
Unless the Lord wills it, of the house as of the city.

So much I have hidden, so much I have buried in you, city of my episcopacy, garden of my generation. Vaults and cisterns echo to my funerals, my inhumations: plots and allotments house my husbanded roots. Men are succeeded by men. Gildo yields to Boniface; but the rooftree does not yield. Across the narrow straits the helmeted and inspired warriors come in their thousands, the Counts of Germany. But Genseric is a man: though his god may be the god of battles, they are battles fought on earth—on dunes, across plains, in dusty streets, among the blood and offal of an earthly topography. Nomads give way to Goths, Goths give way to Vandals. Donatus perished, Pelagius was banished. These things passed: this may also. So much I have hidden, so much I have buried in you, earth of my earth, wonderfully wrought.

In the alleys of Hippo, Freud examines the voided rubbish: the discontents of civilization; the gross matter of dreams. In the forum, the fathers of sociology consult with the fathers of the church. Gibbon and Toynbee measure out their trial-trenches under the olive trees. A sliver of discoloured bone, presumed relic, is borne from Pavia by monks and hutched in Carrara marble below the high altar. Pamphlets and thumbscrews, offprints and imperial insignia descend in volcanic ash on marketplace and harbour, a detritus of theologies, speculations, dogmas. Barbarous manglings, provincial syllogisms. Shelves light with your lucidities, heavy with your superstitions. The tremendous doors of libraries groan on their hinges, plated timbers echo to knocking. But what is opened to us?

I take it up and read it, and I see
Ink and papyrus melt under my gaze.
The verses blur, the luminous syllables
Lapse into darkness. In these latter days
The hills like a broken comb against the light
Scratch at each dawn and dusk, a restless music
Compounded with cicadas, crickets, flies,
Frettings of grasshoppers, the viper's hushed
Swarm down the walls and conduits: siftings, poised
As this whole town is poised, on the edge of silence.

From floor to ceiling, penitential psalms
Repeat their abject praises. Thou, Lord, art just
But justice will be done among men too,
And out beyond the walls and out at sea
Our judges gather to administer it.
Nevertheless, Thy will be done: the church
Fills with your citizens, who will not hear
My voice again, which forty years have brought
To this thin whisper. Silence claims me too.
The shelves of manuscripts entomb my tongue.

The sharp prow rose and fell into the sun,
Carrying me busily on Christ's brisk errands.
Heretics fell in disputation, laws
Were balanced on the scales of my regard.
Now at the jetty no craft waits for me
Or anyone. Again I lift the book,
And close my eyes, and see a city rise
Above all brick and marble ones. Below,
Where men are fearful and their fear is just,
A gorgon mouth yawns open and breathes fire.

L

Stern father, with your unknown face,
Trouble me in whatever place
I try to shun your iron grace.

Curious to know how others live
Yet slow to mend the broken sieve
That is myself, to you I give

Whatever holy residue
Remains of what is good and true.
Keep it, as I come close to you.

It ends.
It is finished.

NOTES

II	'All this goes on inside me, in the vast cloisters of my memory.' *Confessions* X : 8. Thagaste (modern Souk Ahras) was Augustine's birthplace. It lies two hundred miles inland, in what is now Algeria. Its topography is suggested also in Section III.
IV	*'Rationes seminales'*: from *On Genesis*, IX. Some commentators have seen Augustine's remarks about the pattern of change as an anticipation of the theory of evolution.
V–VIII	The Manichees, the Donatists, and the Neo-Platonists all attached great importance to dreams. Augustine was more sceptical: see, for example, *On the Trinity*, XV—'For who does not know that what people see in dreams is precisely like what they see when awake?'
VII	This is an adaptation of one of the 'Fragments' attributed to Petronius (died AD 66). I have no evidence, of course, that Augustine ever read Petronius, but 'old reprobate' (in VIII) would have been a possible way for him to have described the pagan author of *The Satyricon*.
IX	Madaura (modern Mdaourouch) lies about thirty miles south of Thagaste. Augustine was at boarding-school there between the ages of fifteen and sixteen. The ruins of the town are still considerable.
IX and X	'I had prayed to you for chastity and said, "Give me chastity and continence, but not yet." ' *Confessions* VIII : 7.
XI	'I went to Carthage, where I found myself in the midst of a hissing cauldron of lust.' *Confessions* III : 1. Augustine plays, in Latin, on the place-name and on a semi-homonym meaning a type of cooking-pot.
XII	The second part of this section is taken from Lucretius, *Concerning the Nature of Things*, Book I. If Augustine ever read Lucretius, he no doubt disliked him.
XIV	'Thou hast made us for thyself, and our heart is restless until it rests in thee.' *Confessions* I : 1.
XV	Augustine sailed for Rome, by himself, in 383, and spent an unhappy year there. *Confessions* V : 8–12.
XVIII	Symmachus, Prefect of Milan, appointed Augustine as professor of rhetoric for the city in 384. It was Symmachus who once wrote: 'The highroad to office is often laid open by literary success.'
XVIII–XIX	On abstinence, see *Confessions* X : 31.
XX–XXI	'At first the pain was sharp and searing, but then the wound began to fester, and though the pain was duller there was all the less hope of a cure.' *Confessions* VI : 15. The name of

Augustine's mistress is not known. 'She went back to Africa . . .'

XXIII–XXIV *Confessions* VIII : 12. For his *'dolor pectoris'*, see *Confessions* IX : 2.

XXV Augustine experienced his conversion in August 386. He probably began the *Confessions* in 396, when he was forty-two years old.

'the self-portrait of a convalescent': Peter Brown's description of *Confessions* X, in *Augustine of Hippo* (p. 177).

'Peritus . . . periturus': 'I used to talk glibly as though I knew the meaning of it all. . . . Had I continued to be such an expert, I should have died.' *Confessions* VII : 20.

XXVI For the 'innumerable marvels', *The City of God* XXI : 5.

XXVII *'otium liberale'*: cultured retirement; see *Retractions* I : 1, *('Christianae vitae otium')*. Also *Confessions* IX : 4 for Augustine's retreat at Cassiciacum, not far from Lake Como.

XXIX–XXX Augustine was baptized by Ambrose in the baptistry now below Milan Cathedral at Easter 387.

XXXII Augustine returned to Africa to take up his ministry in 388, first to Carthage, then to Thagaste, and finally to Hippo.

XXXIV Needless to say, this 'sermon' is as anachronistic as much else in the present book. Nevertheless, Augustine's *'eruditio'*, *'admonitio'*, and *'disciplina'* are not idly seen as analogous to Mussolini's *'credere'*, *'obbedire'*, and *'combattere'*. For 'the canes of the schoolmasters . . .', see *Confessions* I : 14. For the whole matter of the Donatists and *circumcellions* (here 'vigilantes'), see Peter Brown *op. cit.*, chapters 19–21, and W. H. C. Frend's *The Donatist Church: a movement of protest in Roman North Africa*. 'Know what you are fighting for . . .' is an adaptation of Cromwell's supposed remark on his Ironsides.

XXXV In reply to the 'wild ravings and rantings' of the Donatists, which were frequently cast in the form of popular songs, Augustine himself did in fact compose an 'A.B.C. against the Donatists': the refrain to the third stanza is taken from it.

XXXVI 'Filled with fear . . .': from a sermon by Augustine on the text 'Do not be slow to turn to the Lord, nor delay from day to day, for his wrath shall come when you know not.'

XXXVIII In 410, the Emperor Honorius ordered a debate to be held between the Donatists and the Catholics, led by Augustine. This took place at the great baths in Carthage in June 411. Augustine triumphed: 'Let falsehood . . .' was the judgement of Flavius Marcellinus, who presided over the debate.

XL One could think of Faustus the Manichee and of Pelagius, among other apologists and moralists.

XLI	The worship of Baal, Tanit, and other Punic deities was common among the pagans of Numidia.
XLII	'a stone salt-glazed jar': see Ralph Merrifield's 'The Use of Bellarmines as Witch-Bottles', *The Guildhall Miscellany*, no. 3, February 1954.
XLIII	*'Unde hoc malum?'*: see *Augustine of Hippo*, p. 394. For the potter's wheel, *Lamentations* 4 : 2 is one of a number of Biblical references.
	'The cricket chirps . . .': said by Eraclius, Augustine's own appointed successor as Bishop of Hippo, in his first sermon in 426.
XLVI	Rome fell to Alaric and his Gothic army in August 410. Many refugees fled to Africa.
XLVII	Gildo, the Moorish Count of Africa, usurped Numidia in the late fourth century, until he was suppressed by the Emperor Honorius. Boniface, at the head of Gothic troops, had become Count of Africa by 423. Genseric, King of the Vandals, completed the subjugation of Roman Africa during the next decade.
XLVIII	The only tangible relic of Augustine is a fragment of arm bone, brought from Pavia to the Basilica of Hippo in the nineteenth century and placed inside a marble effigy of Augustine behind the high altar, where it remains to this day.
XLIX	During his final illness, Augustine ordered 'the four psalms of David that deal with penance' to be copied out and hung on the walls of his room. He died on 28 August 430. A year later Hippo was sacked.